HAVE YOU SEEN THIS MAN?

Have You Seen This Man? The Castro Poems of Karl Tierney
Arkansas Queer Poet Series #2

Copyright © 2019 by the Literary Estate of Karl Tierney

Cover photograph and "Missing" poster provided by the Literary Estate of Karl Tierney

Cover design by Seth Pennington

Sibling Rivalry Press, LLC
PO Box 26147
Little Rock, AR 72221

info@siblingrivalrypress.com

www.siblingrivalrypress.com

ISBN: 978-1-943977-68-0

Library of Congress Control No. 2019938609

By special invitation, this title is housed in the Rare Book and Special Collections Vault of the Library of Congress.

First Sibling Rivalry Press Edition, October 2019

ARKANSAS
QUEER POET
SERIES
#2

HAVE YOU SEEN THIS MAN?

THE CASTRO POEMS OF
KARL TIERNEY

EDITED BY JIM CORY

SIBLING RIVALRY PRESS

DISTURB/ENRAPTURE

LITTLE ROCK, ARKANSAS

FOR ALL THE BOYS WHO JUMPED TO LIVE

CONTENTS

AN INTRODUCTION
by Jim Cory

"No one is forgotten, nothing is forgotten."
– Olga Bergholz

At the time I met him, in 1987, Karl Tierney had two things on his mind: finding love and writing great poetry.

He'd landed in San Francisco four years earlier, after completing an MFA degree at the University of Arkansas in Fayetteville. In the City by the Bay, he was convinced both these ambitions would be fulfilled.

As to love, what could be more certain? In 1983, the year he arrived, the Castro neighborhood was a city within a city, teeming with gay men in their 20s and 30s. It had a certain testosterone vibe, offering limitless amorous opportunity.

Regarding Karl's literary ambition, what better place could there be to bring it to fruition? With its Berkeley Renaissance tradition of the 40s and 50s, its famous City Lights Books, its beatniks of the past and resident luminaries such as Michael McClure, Gary Snyder, Philip Whalen, Joanne Kyger, William Everson, Thom Gunn, and many more, it boasted a literary culture second only to New York's.

Yet, as Karl moved to pursue poetry in a serious way—he calls it, in one poem, "my vocation"—there was little discernible influence on it or in it by any of those people.

Actually, the two writers whose thought and spirit leave some traces in Karl's poetry had absolutely nothing to do with San Francisco.

13

The first is Frank O'Hara. The debt's not obvious, but it's there, firstly in a stance, which combines artistic and historical erudition with street smarts to chronicle the everyday. It's there in the exclamation points—bane of creative writing courses—that come often and sometimes thick. ("It is Monet who led us astray!") Like O'Hara, the voice is both casual and intense. The poems sometimes sound like someone sharing a confidence with intimates, at other times they could be rants delivered across a café table. Much of their subject matter—cruising, dating, soggy overnight assignations, fumbling attempts at relationships and the recriminations that often follow—concerns the search for erotic satisfaction, if not connection:

> *Nothing's incessant but lust with so many*
> *beautiful young lollipops and white-meat thighs.*
> "Bed Making"

These are also, many of them, poems of place. Whether it's twinks skipping down Market Street ("Skippy") or punk rockers off on a gleeful farting spree through the Haight ("Letting Air"), they vibrate with the joy of just being in that most beautiful and magical of American cities. Not the gentrified, tech-mad San Francisco of the present, but the San Francisco that existed before the Dot-Com boom started driving up real estate prices and rents in the mid-'90s, and even prior, in the early '80s, just before anyone really knew how many had been infected with the HIV virus, something that would be clear soon enough.

Oh what a paradise it was. Frances FitzGerald notes in *Cities on a Hill*, her book on visionary communities, that while many an American metropolis had gay bars or even a gay neighborhood, and some had had them for decades, the Castro was something qualitatively different. Starting in the mid-'70s, thousands of gay men from all over America—in effect, runaways from a Puritan sexual ethos—moved to that corner of San Francisco at the far west end of Market Street. Before *Will & Grace*, before *Lawrence v. Texas* or gay marriage, they transformed what had been a mostly white working-class community into a vibrant "out" enclave, with its own politics, institutions, media and vibe.

Their descent on San Francisco, FitzGerald notes, resembled the movement a decade or so prior when college students and teenagers—also runaways—had swarmed into Haight-Ashbury for the Summer of Love.

Speed and heroin undid Haight-Ashbury. The Castro, in all its sexual exuberance, lasted a bit longer. Today both are tour bus destinations for middle-class curiosity seekers. But even then the "gay mecca" drew its share of tourists, a fact that inspires vexatious quips at a number of points in these poems.

What caused the Castro to unravel, of course, was AIDS. In tracing that process, FitzGerald records the following: "In San Francisco, one of the cities where the disease was first noticed, there were 24 cases in December 1981, 61 cases six months later and 118 cases the following December—and so on."

Besides multiplying exponentially, AIDS was nearly always fatal. Between 1981, when the Centers for Disease Control and Prevention first gave it a name, and early 1996, when a class of antiretroviral drugs known as protease inhibitors offered the first effective treatment, the average life expectancy between diagnosis and death was 18 months, usually wretched ones.

The disease decimated first individuals, then a community. Thousands died—"20,000 is the estimate for San Francisco, most of them gay men, most of them decades too soon," *San Francisco Chronicle* health reporter Erin Allday wrote in 2016. That time frame in the city's history—1981 to 1996—roughly overlaps the period when Karl Tierney lived there.

★ ★ ★

Merriam-Webster defines fate as "the will or principle or determining cause by which things in general are believed to come to be as they are or events to happen as they do."

Its closest synonym? Destiny. Corresponding, the Greeks believed, to cosmic order in action.

When Karl arrived in 1983, AIDS was still a scary sort of rumor, involving friends-of-friends-of-friends. As months and then years swept by, it became the dominant social fact, liable to emerge in any conversation. Those flying in from outside, who thought we had an idea of what was going on, were soon enough disabused.

On a visit in the late '80s, a San Francisco friend tells me he's tested negative for HIV.

"You must be relieved," I say.

"I told my best friend. He burst into tears," he says, shaking his head.

"But why?"

"He said I was the only person he knew who'd tested negative for the virus."

Once on a separate visit, also in the late '80s, I sit down in Café Flore (see "Café Hairdo") to read the *San Francisco Bay Guardian*. One full page consists of pictures of men in their 20s, 30s, and 40s next to small blocks of text in inky type. This gives pause. I flip it to find a two-page facing spread of similar obits. Then another. Then another.

On a third visit, in October of 1989, I stroll down Divisadero one Saturday morning around 10 AM to find, piled on the sidewalk at Castro and 18th, a wall of cages. Cats and dogs stare, each wet nose at the wire available for adoption.

So pervasive was viral infection by then that many long-time Castro residents were viewing the situation fatalistically, a point of view present in Karl Tierney's poems such as "Dating in a Thinning Field," where the double entendre of the title aims to wring wit from all this and, if that doesn't succeed, there's the irony of pretending to lament the dwindling number of available potential partners:

> *The good ones have died*
> *or can't afford a face-lift*
> *and won't answer the phone.*
>   "Dating in a Thinning Field"

Yet even in the face of relentless death and disease, life in the Castro went on. Guys still dated, though the first question on any outing was likely to be: What's your HIV status? They went to the baths (see "The Steam Room") or to dance clubs ("Like the Clap or Some Chronic Disease"), even to swimming pool parties ("Adonis at the Swimming Pool"). This is the way the world ends. This is the way the world ends. This is the way the world ends.

★ ★ ★

That documenting the disintegration of this demimonde became Karl's project was an accident, the writer's response to changed historical circumstance. History offers analogies. One would be Olga Bergholz, who never ceased writing and broadcasting her poems during the 872 days Hitler's army laid siege to Leningrad.

That this could even happen largely owes to the development, at that point, of gay poetry as a genre. Two decades before—let's say 1965—writing poems that celebrate or even assume same-sex affection would've been largely unthinkable outside a certain avant-garde, i.e. Robert Duncan, Allen Ginsberg, Jack Spicer, et al. By the time AIDS arrives, that's changed. Magazines devoted to gay writing—*Christopher Street*, *The James White Review*, and *modern words*—flourished. Their success prepared the ground for broader acceptance of such work. Karl's poem "June 21, 1989," for instance, first appeared in *American Poetry Review*:

> *Still, what's left is most attractive to me,*
> *which means I'm horny, which is most dangerous*
> *these days, in this era of No One's Choosing.*
> "June 21, 1989"

By this time, say around 1990, the voice has come fully into its own. It's confident and direct, even while embodying all the poet's emotional contradictions, being both hopeful and bitter, disappointed and glad. It's also ironic, cutting, and sometimes even cruel in a catty way. Nothing unusual there. If you were seated in the adjoining booth at a coffee shop after the gay AA meeting on 18th Street, or eavesdropping on a trio of queens in some corner of the Midnight Sun, across the street, conversation would move along similar lines.

The poetry experiments where and when it needs to. It's frank rather than confessional, since confession is a sentimental manipulation of frankness, and Karl's instincts as a poet were usually sound. Sometimes it reveals an unseemly side that, in person, would most likely have been masked. The essential tools were in the box when he'd arrived. Now there are more, and he knows how to use them.

★ ★ ★

What's surprising about the Castro in the '80s and '90s was that, even with AIDS decimating its population, the search for love scarcely slackened. If a gay man couldn't find love in that gayest of gay neighborhoods, where would he ever find it? If anything, the search becomes yet more obsessive, since settling down with a boyfriend, in some presumably monogamous situation, represents, like abstinence, one kind of salvation. But old ways make it hard to pull off:

> *I would not mind so much*
> *if tonight you'd call*
> *with those toxic charms*
> *my friends hear too much of.*
>   "The Blindness of Habit"

Love is the most complicated human emotion because it contains, actually or potentially, all others. With it, you can bear almost any difficulty or inconvenience. Without it, life often becomes a shell.

This explains the relentless search, with death now its backdrop. It makes rational the logic of all the self-defeating behavior Karl observes and describes. Typically, that once-scrawny queen in "Bodybuilder" recreates himself pumping iron in empty Saturday night gyms, only to become "a powerhouse of loneliness."

You have to wonder. If AIDS had never arrived, would this sexual Utopia have imploded anyway? It seems, also alluded to here, that that process was already underway; the plague only accelerates it:

> *It's not easy to propel one's spirit through this*
> *nocturnal society ruled by the hard wit of seminary dropouts*
> *cutting for advantage.*
>   "The Acquisition of Nothing"

No doubt. Or was it simply that Karl had arrived at a conclusion many gay men reach, which is that simply finding your way into this world of like-minded beings, which in the '70s and even in the '80s took some work to do, guarantees no satisfaction in and of itself? Queens will be queens, which means that some can be selfish, manipulative, back-stabbing, dishonest, even monsters, like the drunken bar rag editor in "Sot," crossing names off his enemies list as he checks the obituaries.

This was a shock I suspect Karl never quite fully absorbed: "I've been talking with my therapist about how I think gay men are mean to one another, or simply mean," he wrote me, in a letter dated Oct. 27/28, 1993, "and this increases with each year of the plague—more self-loathing. Never right enough, never good enough. As children we either get bullied (or we imagine we do or we just fear we will). Then we spend the rest of our lives throwing barbs at one another, 'bitchy,' 'camp,' 'catty,' whatever (of course, the feminized terms!). It's wanting to bully back. Poetry is a good art form for presenting this in succinct, laconic epigrams, and there's a long tradition of that."

★ ★ ★

One of that tradition's most prominent exponents is Gaius Valerius Catullus (84 BC-54 BC). The bard from Verona similarly exercised a wit of such unsparing honesty and vitality that 20 or so centuries on we still crack up at his zingers.

Here is the other writer whose ghost we find moving across these pages. For Catullus, Karl's admiration was unabashed. "Whore," for instance—"you are I believe the kept boy/of that fat pig Wharton"—is "after Catullus." After? He's channeling him. The method is direct address, the victim presumably alive to read it:

My friend Chuck, you spend your energies
envying the lover of beautiful blond Dane.
In your loneliness, you dwell on what you lack.
                                              "Envy"

As with the Roman poet, ardor and spite, sometimes combined ("Litany on a Perfect Ass"), animate the text. Rivals, ex-lovers ("Boyfriend Artiste"), and overnight sexual guests all get whacked:

> *Totally cool, relaxed,*
> *almost studiously ill-mannered,*
> *he goes through my pockets*
> *with the curiosity of a gypsy...*
> "The Thief"

The fun in reading is watching sincerity transformed into ridicule. The community ("Christmas Party Above the Castro") and its various institutions ("The Steam Room" or "Club Uranus"), similarly, all take their hits.

The Catullus connection also makes yet more relevant the analogy Karl repeatedly drew between Rome in its late period decadence and America in the immediate post-Vietnam period, a place of debt-driven consumerism wanting in all taste. When it comes to spiritual satisfaction, this national "bourgeois logjam of more upon more" proves a chimera, much as San Francisco finally proved to be when it came to the search for love. In that search, Karl was as much Tantalus as he was Catullus, the water level in the stream falling even as he bent to drink, the branch heavy with ripe fruit bending back, somehow, ever beyond his grasp. Yet, like any good comedian, he found a way—specifically in irony—to make his disappointments the source of amusement. He had learned that to mock anyone or anything with effect, you must first learn by practicing on yourself.

★ ★ ★

Thirteen years pass between the poet's arrival in San Francisco in 1982 and his death in October of 1995. The immediate cause of that death was suicide, but what triggered the decision to take his own life was disease. He had been actively AIDS symptomatic since December of 1994. Deeply depressed and knowing too well what the disease looked like as it progressed, he got on his bike, rode to the Golden Gate Bridge, and climbed up and over the rail.

As you may gather, the poetry—which begins in a basic sort of graduate school competence—progresses in time to something much more. Sometime after 1990, the line loosens up, the images sharpen. In "Clone Nouveau" or "Why I Don't Live There" you can feel the poise. It's evident in the way the poet takes on big new themes or, in revisiting familiar ground ("Hangover"), pushes the poem deeper.

Part of this is talent rising to the challenge of its subject. It is also the product of a certain diligence. His meticulous manuscript files reveal the process. The poems begin as crude blocks of words scribbled in ballpoint, and move from there to the typewriter. Each has its file folder. The sheafs of dated drafts reveal that they seldom took less than a year, and often as long as five, to find finished form. He labored on a dozen or so at a time and kept as many as ten manuscripts circulating to magazines. Fifty-two poems appeared in print in his lifetime. He was a finalist once for the National Poetry Series and twice for the Walt Whitman Award, given by the Academy of American Poets to a first book.

This devoted attention stops, for the most part, with the onset of illness. As 1995 progressed, he essentially ceased writing or revising poems. (The last drafts in most of his files date to March 18, 1995, the last poem here to May 13, 1995.) He'd left his job and was becoming progressively sicker, though exactly in what ways he did not reveal in the letters he wrote at this time. What I found out later was that in the early fall of that year, he had, through his doctor, applied for inclusion in a trial group for protease inhibitors, and been told, when the application was processed, that he was not qualified.

The silence about his illness lasted until September 7, when a penciled note arrives. It reads: "I need to be really brief because there seems like so much to do and I'm feeling overwhelmed. My health is deteriorating and at this point looking real bad, the outlook I mean. I am asking you to be my literary executor for my poems, particularly in terms of editing and publishing any future manuscripts posthumously…"

Five weeks later he disappeared. Someone found his bike parked by the bridge. When his parents entered Karl's apartment, they found his wallet, driver's license, and a final note lying on the kitchen table. Among the messages recorded on his answering machine was one from his doctor, saying a mistake had been made in evaluating his application and that he was, in fact, eligible to participate in the protease inhibitor trial. No body was recovered.

★ ★ ★

The publication of these poems almost a quarter century after Karl Tierney's death is a rarity in the world of letters: a volume by a writer whose work, in his own lifetime, never actually appeared in book form. That this poetry could not just quietly disappear into dumpster or file drawer speaks to the spirit and quality it contains.

HAVE YOU SEEN THIS MAN?

DRESSING

My eyes are blue in the morning,
green by the end of the day's teasing.
"Blue the better shade," I think.
What a thick head on these silly shoulders!
For months I've lived with myself
stuck before the mirror after dinner.
Ah, that look of sad sincerity
and those Belgian corduroys!
Dashing, but one cannot dash about the bars
of current San Francisco in such attire.
One must be droll or caught by the troll!
The Magic Mirror gestures and says,
"Go for the balls!"
Gray has not the slightest chance this night.
But a touch of red and heap of oil may do.

October 29, 1983

OUT ON THE STREETS AND SIMPLY RUNNING INTO EX-LOVERS

This is not an ordinary night.
They are out tonight like driving rain.
It is Halloween, everyone else it seems
feels giddy in capes, low-cal beer,
and too much mascara.
You get caught with ketchup on your heart
    and your waist wrapped tight.
Your night howls with black cats
    enraged that two coarse paths cross.
Ex-lovers look steel-cold as yuppies
    or rattle a little like machines still loose.
Suddenly, they purr sorry, want to
    "be friends," come on as cute.
You might even laugh but no one
    has seen your face in seven months
    and your mouth (always small)
    has vanished from disuse.
All in all, it's a fair deal.
Call it God-given, call it gratitude.

Freedom just around the corner,
but the eyes of ex-lovers stick like glue.
You never did learn to hold them nude,
    now they want to hold you, wasted.
It may be ten o'clock.
It may be midnight.
Too late for incidentals,
    there's nothing left to do.

December 7, 1985

JAPAN

*Beauty, beautiful things, those
are now my most deadly enemies.*
　　　　　　　　—*Yukio Mishima*

Rigid and serious, its staccato brilliance
is now immersed in commerce
so that from out of hallowed
traditions of self-destruction
emerges a merely would-be suicide
who makes an art of it
then sells it to the world like glue.
More fastidious when stark with poverty,
now the Curse of the Green Snake
is wrapped around its heart
like seaweed around sushi.
Silently the Japanese remember
Pearl, Wake, the Bomb.
Something simmers in the pot.

I am with my friend Jack.
We sip ice-cold Coca-Cola
at a drive-in near Nara,
the ancient imperial capital
now surrounded by junkyards and daisies
where peasants once grew straw
to make their own tea.
We bow to each other,
then sip from the same Coke.
Our love is built by Mitsubishi.

March 15, 1986

BILLY IDOL'S BIRTHDAY

Too much leather melts the ice cream.

When we crack, we crack
like cane too laden with sugar
so that we fall severely
(weak-kneed and stomach-wrenched).
We fall at the third blow.
Our wishes unravel a string of pain.
Our beautiful blond hair starts to stick
to the brush. It comes out in tufts.
We scan the mirror for an inkling,
which flaw, which disease.
We have been tortured with "bad boy" syndromes.
Once wrapped in sheets still steamy from bodies
gone from the orgy, our rejection is eternal.
Our mothers do not call.
We have little left but asylums,
drug rehabilitation centers,
dark bushes in parks in which
to hide and curse ourselves.

April 23, 1986

BEAUTY

It comes at you from nowhere
and has the disturbing quality
of knowing your desire

On occasion it appears nude in your bed
you can even touch it and more
and then it's off hiring a lawyer
or was only a dream in the first place

Perhaps it's in West Hollywood shopping
or standing still on a sidewalk
with only a hand in motion
hitchhiking its way to Bel Air

December 12, 1986

WHORE
after Catullus

O glamorous whore!
with bone for an ass
and a stub for a nose
banal fingers
filthy ears and inane eyes
overextended credit
and the heightened diction
of a salesman
you are I believe the kept boy
of that fat pig Wharton.

And the City calls you gorgeous.
They set you up beside my Jerome.
O generation drunken and blind!

June 6, 1987

PART-TIME WHORES IN DOORWAYS

Some of them are handsome,
even if two sheets to the wind

shaking skin and bones.
Little meat upon them

except between the legs
meticulously exposed when rising

toward tweaks, Johns, or numbers.
There is no need for pity.

They milk even the bosom of Mary
and display the kind of rage

that always gets attention.
While the rest of us,

with a pocket full of
sweetness, flirt with danger

as if we were simply rescuing
Baby Moses from a reed basket.

June 6, 1987

GERTRUDE STEIN TO ALICE B. TOKLAS

We are fast.
We are fast driving.
Lands unknown.
We are fast driving for lands unknown to us.
Our car.
Our car is a Packard.
Our car is a beautiful blue Packard convertible
  and we are fast driving.
Our car is ours, not the bank's,
  and is beautiful and blue
  and we are beautiful and not blue
  and we are fast driving
  and do not feel a bit dangerous or dirty.
We have the radio on
  and then do not.
First we have the radio on, for the music
  and then we have it off, for the silence.
No! Silence is a lie
  for there is always wind.
We have the sound of wind
  so silence is a lie
  when we have the radio off.
In the wind is your red scarf
  and our car is a Packard.
A Packard. Yes, a Packard
  and your red scarf is moving in the wind
  in our beautiful blue Packard convertible.
Your red scarf is moving
  for we are fast driving
  towards lands that do not
  give us a clue of what they might hold.

Fast, yes, fast driving we are
  in a beautiful blue Packard,
  but are neither blue nor worried
  nor very dangerous nor dirty, really.
We are merely fast
  and can be heard with the radio off
  in the sound of the wind.

June 29, 1987

THE BLINDNESS OF HABIT

I would not mind so much
if tonight you'd call
with those toxic charms
my friends hear too much of.
You'd wear an outrageous hat
and steer me into the cityscape
with hearty tavern laughter
till dawn when I'd waken
dizzy and sick
the night a foolish blur
the joy flushed down the toilet
and, with no money left,
curse the sun's damn glare.

August 10, 1987

ARKANSAS LANDSCAPE: WISH YOU WERE HERE

for Frank O'Hara

It's windy outside,
and red-nosed boys from the hills
walk free from sin-shod shoes
through the collegetown mall.
Everywhere there's hair blowing
(brown mostly)
and the bushes huddle together
animated in conversations about the sea,
what it might be.
They gather that it's full of weeds
and smells.
Here and there those long skirts fly,
and the loud of car radios
presses through the blows.
It's Wednesday outside,
which is, of course, wonderful
and the secrets of the world
are unraveling here.

August 27, 1987

THE THIEF

He sits stiff as Lincoln
on my Salvation Army chair
in the abattoir of my Bohemia
ablaze with flaw.
His crotch warrants itself
unwiped from his last meal,
doubtlessly a part
of my initial attraction.

Totally cool, relaxed,
almost studiously ill-mannered,
he goes through my pockets
with the curiosity of a gypsy
and the justifiable resentment
of one who sailed all this way
with only half a mast
to begin with.

                              August 28, 1987

ADONIS AT THE SWIMMING POOL

Who dances his thighs across the pool's water,
 spread on a mattress bloated from his breath.

Whose ripe-with-sun skin cuts through the spray
 with the alingual grace of a kiss to my brow.

Whose blue eyes flash from under torrents
 and swim my way so wretched in wanting.

Who sips from a warm cocktail as if
 it were Arctic ice splendid in summer.

Who minds not my advantageous looks,
 my devious plots and debonair waves,
 but weighs them for their worth in flattery.

Whose wet curls stroke the evening's earliest gasp
 into naughty tones and murmurs of lust.

Who would have me discussed in seedy cafés
 and ruin me since I'm deaf to the hiss
 behind the teeth in that insipid smile.

August 28, 1987

THE STRIPPER

Stuck in a Central Valley bar
while San Francisco fiddles on water
(I could be vicious in the reviews!)
I buzz through your performance
busy as an expert in sleaze
who decides to rate you highly
and is very pleased with himself.
Here (Merced, Modesto, Fresno),
reduced to good teeth, immortal thighs,
and a G-string tucked with $5 bills,
the toast of mediocrity.

Gracious or desperate,
you mingle after the show.
I buy you a sneering drink,
say I'm from San Francisco,
which, here, is like saying
I could make you a big star.
You can't take your eyes off the mirrors.
So what do you think about
the still-lingering threat
of fascism in Greece, I say,
returning the naked cruelty.

August 28, 1987

TURNING 30

By 30, one discovers there's no age
when one doesn't feel awkward,
just as one finds Great Causes
cannot be swallowed whole,
and no one kisses so divinely
the second time.

What a sign of maturity
to be indifferent to bullying at bus stops or
the bad breath of ogres who like our wounds!
To jog through Nature with the radio on,
certain that something is familiar but unable
to put its lousy foot forward and shake hands.

We convince ourselves
that Success is a fair trade for Youth.
Pretty Narcissus, petty and vain.
Now there's crow's feet and wisdom
over choosing asparagus spears at the Super
and the Plymouth finally sold
to someone just past half our age
eager to part with what little he has.

August 28, 1987

SUICIDE OF A VIDEO HEAD

"They are called *photos*.
Paintings are *pictures*."

"Some shit this is," you said.
A few of your photos published
in a couple of throwaway mags
run by pickpocket editors
        who still tremble from the Cold War.
As if you and a million other good photographers
could take over the galleries
and actually sell something artistic
to tourists who fly in for postcards
or pay rent by shooting stupid fashion shows
or "break into" the big one, *Life*.

So you ventured into something marketable,
videos(!), bought into the hysteria
that hi-tech will save the Empire,
thought Hollywood would grab you up,
like you just dropped from the womb, dude.
In June you threw a fabulous Selling Out party
full of fabulous A-One people
        who sold out from the get-go
        who maybe had no choice.

No problem,
until you got laid off
the same day your A-One lover
laid your replacement
and you put yourself blue and cold
into a warm bath.

With whiskey and pills, and no note,
no accusations, no angry Anarchist bombs,
you went like a bony horse
that plops in the trough after
so many years of iron love and labor
and the free world moving
fucking fast.

I met you during The Transition phase,
from f-stop to ASA to fast-forward,
wondered, Is it real or is it Memorex?
Your Castro apartment is now a tourist hotel.
Your best, those framed black and whites, are gone.
I still have the punk sunglasses that date you.
I still owe you dinner at Neon Chicken.

Now I tell grand lies on a chaise lounge
        like The Last Emperor
        I am either a survivor or a killer
        drinking immunity-building O.J.
        reading *The New Yorker* gloriously
        dreaming of something consequential
        that changes my life too, dude.
But when I feel like writing fiction,
I just take a nap.

                            March 1, 1988

SUMMER SOLSTICE

The fool you met last night,
when a risky wind pushed you
into his orbit, has gathered
his seedy self from your bed.
Exiled to the garden,
he's bent over
growing hemorrhoids
while he paws the cat
and smiles vapidly
in the direction of our kitchen,
which is far too yellow.

You might as well operate an inn!
So you wear a flashy maroon robe
your mother sent last Christmas
while you squeeze fresh orange juice,
crack the eggs, melt the butter.
What a relief, you think,
the nights are short
this time of year,
and the light will drive
foreigners from the land.

March 4, 1988

THREE PUNKS AMONG THE '80S MASSES

The three untouchables
must think it's Easter,
in pink hats, bunny ears,
hair of green and jaundiced eyes
that brim with Christian charity.
They look like anarcho-syndicalists
would on *Star Trek*,
Don Knotts in leather but thinner.

A night out, popping Molotovs.
A short line to snort at 6 AM,
a girl corpse
naked in the dumpster,
back of the park?
They do it all,
then leave their scent.
Me, on the other hand, the big
risk I take is having a cola
then a cigarette or two
while doing the Twist
in a clean, well-lighted place
with some yo-yo.

                                        November 22, 1988

JACKIE O

Every century you get a new facelift
just like Venice, Europe.
Then there you go again
isolating and rude,
denying us even a photograph.

We want to see your cesarean scars.
We want to make a Smithsonian exhibit out of you
climbing on the trunk of a Lincoln convertible.
We want your luncheon remains
with that saliva on it he kissed
or his dry-cleaned brains on that pink suit.
We don't ask what we could do for you
but what you can do for us.
Grant an interview to *Interview*.
Tell us we're selfish.
Tell us we stink.
Tell us we're not like you.

November, 1988

CLONE NOUVEAU

So   like
like I'm coming out of Au Natural drinking my Hercules Flip
and get scared
think I see   one person   simultaneously as two
ya know   like
                        I'm cross-eyed or something
one to my left   one to my right
cloned from the horn-rim glasses   to the Italian shoes
even with my Panavision and quick thinking
this is almost too much to gauge
I mean the very shock of it
        all the 70s clone types dead
and this
        in the midst of my mourning
something utterly new in fashion
if not philosophy   and the difficulty
of so much to register utterly all at once
no doubt   a vitamin deficiency

So   like   backing up
                                    once upon a time
        an original had itself   cloned
                    which is like procreating but not
But can they both play chess?
the one obviously in control
                        is obviously the original
                                obviously
                    the one who once
            was alone, got lonely, then cloned

So   like   the original goes toward the other

47

                                        its creature
                                        its offspring
and crosses my path
(bad luck, I'm wearing black)
            and places this life-like mannequin
I refuse to be spellbound by it
or describe it as *lovely*
            on the back of a blue scooter
                  putters off into four lanes of traffic

To catch my breath   I need   a metaphor
      an archetype for referral   a school of thought
a precedent not too bright   with clarity
I think of King Elvis who colored
      the hair of his lovely queen   Priscilla
      blue-black   same as his
      chose her panties   presumably not
      the same as his
                        and
                        when then she
      finally let her own roots grow out
            he decreed   they couldn't go on
            together   with suspicious minds
            and exiled himself
            became a mere hitchhiker
            something like the rest of us
            in the cold Kentucky rain

                              September 13, 1989

MISSION DOLORES

Thank God I wasn't a sexpot.
All the sexpots are dead, or about to be.
— Myrna Loy

Of course there was a scene from *Vertigo* filmed there
when Kim Novak comes and stands in the garden and is
Kim Novak who's had an obsessed Jimmy Stewart
following her, which is not too comfortable, but at least
she's in a Jaguar while being followed, so it could be worse
like having to say *I can't afford that*
or Hitchcock obsessing on what's for lunch after the cut
and the interminable trudging out of young blondes
for modeling under porticoes or rose-covered pergolas
with no dialogue just the visual
in black and white
and the making of fantasy as part of history
never mind that the Indian-killer Father Serra
laid the first stone in 1776
what a fucking year
which is much like everyone today saying
I was first exposed to the virus in 1980
and now Serra's verging on canonization, which only means
that to get into the garden during hours, one continuously
deals with tourists in shorts and cheap cameras
perpetually embarrassing themselves and unconscious
because what really happened here was that
the world was allowed to worship a Goddess of Vanity
which was the truth Hitchcock brought here one morning
in the midst of a mass Denial that continues
with this tremendous erasure
no plaque, no photo, no mention

of Miss Novak's career before her recent
The Mirror Cracked and *Falcon Crest* comeback
is something like confusing starlets of the '50s
with blonde Protestant singers of the '60s
such as Miss Dusty "Wishin' and Hopin'" Springfield
who also sang "Son of a Preacher Man"
but is taken off the shelf like a new discovery with no prior history
when at 48 she records a song with the Pet Shop Boys
that goes all the way to No. 2.
or believing that the good ones are ones like Brigitte Bardot
who go away to nurse calves for an eternity
in the South of France near Avignon.

The mythology derived from the symbol might be an illusion
but not the reality in the fact that *Thank God and thank you*
General Motors Cadillacs are getting bigger again
so that this dreadful era becomes reminiscent of the '50s
as if escape were indeed possible
as I walk by the Mission's garden and all at once a stiff breeze
affects even my pompadour stiff with pomade
and from out of the fog a long black Cadillac passes me by
and I needn't wonder if inside the body is still alive.

September 17, 1989

JUNE 21, 1989

I'm not at my best, and so
it's dangerous to my reputation
to be out tonight in latest twilight
when the vampires are just getting up
and I haven't had a beauty rest in centuries.
Still, I've consumed so much coffee and nonsense
I'm near ecstatic that the longest day of the year
falls on a Wednesday
and not only is it six days past my birthday
but I'm 33 and *pat on the back* sure don't look it.
Who could possibly want to? As if that's
some kind of accomplishment beyond
a combination of genetics and fear.
And the earth has shifted once again today
on its axis. All of which is to say
it's a fine line between anger and depression
when I've gone from overeating to gorgeously starved
in just one season, in time for summer colors, though
"free will" means there is no choice and I must daily
force myself not just into satins but into black
in a city too sophisticated for guilt and shame
where death is an obsession and the panhandlers
do crossword puzzles and street musicians play Mozart
and "the exceptionally good looking" who once stepped
off into a Cadillac, Mercedes, stretch Lincoln, Bentley, Rolls,
have met their sunset, yet I'm out, like I just ejaculated
from a toaster, having come to loathe the sun
which is the key to immortality if the visual
reigns supreme and everyone's dying to be seen.
Those with too many resentments simply explode.
The streets clog with the usual Leftist litter,

sidewalks with shorts, sunglasses, the smell of pomade,
sewers with the beady-eyed scurry of plague.
Still, what's left is most attractive to me,
which means I'm horny, which is most dangerous
these days, in this era of No One's Choosing.

September 22, 1989

AT PETER'S PLACE

How oft does the life of Petros fill with chaos!
15-year-olds wallow in bed the day long.
This is not a throne a pope could rule from!
Too many voices of infallibility drown
in the ambiguities of the toilet's flush.
Call in the Anglicans!
17-year-olds roller skate across Kurdistans and Persians.
The Afghans are tied up in mothballs.
The Frigidaire offers little more than liver pâté.
The kitty kicks up her skirt along the kitchen walls.
It is Monet that led us astray!
Sometimes it is Hell to maintain control.
The Semblance of Order fails upon the divan.
Dishes pile up in the sink.
The lady downstairs dying, bangs her cane.
Sometimes I too shoot at the Stars.
Everyone is out to make his mark, to be heard.

January 3, 1990

JUSTINIAN

Franks to the north,
and Vandals to the south.

Visigoths to the west
and Ostrogoths all around.

But thanks to your purity, Justinian,
still no sign of the Vulgars!

March 8, 1990

DATING IN A THINNING FIELD

The same pattern finds itself fulfilled.
I slip into something more comfortable.
Then the real discomfort begins.
That low self-esteem won't rub off
while once again I must converse
with creatures from Planet Z
who've come to earth
to partake in the fast-feed frenzy
that occupies this century.
The good ones have died
or can't afford a face-lift
and won't answer the phone.

August 4, 1990

POSTCARDS FROM ABROAD

I.

My horoscope says watch for an authority figure
who will give me something. But fate
tends toward tardiness, and meanwhile
what do I know of shipments
in exchange for hostages
or arms in exchange for loneliness?
I cannot begin to pronounce the names
of Persian port cities much less get laid
without having my billfold gone through.

II.

Greetings from Monte Carlo
and Grace Kelly off the cliff in a Rover!
Not that I'm mad at you,
just had to get away and into the world
while still young, et cetera, nothing lasts,
which is the beauty of it.
Don't be angry, instead remember your
"generous heart," as you once put it.
Now, it's someone else's turn
at the wheel.

III.

I must tell you, I lied.
Everything is not okay,
my disturbance deeper than anxiety.
I'm afraid of owing the world something.

From the picture you can see his tomb.
Paris so grand, but all roads
lead to Rome, making a neat seam.

IV.

Rang up Luigi, you'd said "Likes Americans."
Drove to Pisa in his Cadillac listening
to that tape by In Pursuit of Happiness.
He got stoned. I looked out the window
at the changing landscape. He became
very animated, wants you to know
he especially likes "I'm an Adult Now."
You are so big, like pop culture
you can reach me anywhere.
And the *Tower*? Looks like it leans on air,
a trick I'd like to learn.

V.

Forget the picture, old,
it's of Pompeii.
Now I'm in Messina, Sicily,
a city without postcards!
Not used to tourists, dark and friendly
but poor and would like money
and I'm running out.
I'm reminded of the time,
something particularly innocuous on TV,
I asked what you thought caused
Rome to fall. *The loss of cheap labor*,
you said.

VI.

I saw your eyes in the brothels of Tangier.
Oops! Wrong century. All right, then
I like to think of you as my Eva Braun
during her last stay at Berchtesgaden
taking perennially-constipated Blondi
on long strolls with Speer,
obsessed with the increasing difficulty
in acquiring good cosmetics.

VII.

Dear Terezin

    I'm fine. The air smells
    fresh here. Am sleeping in
    till 10 every morning.
    Tomorrow tea with our comrade Z_____
    whose health is even better than mine.
    Must run. Late for aerobics.

        —[Auschwitz] [Oswiecim]

           October 28, 1990

LETTING AIR

Today, all along Haight Street
punk-rock girls are letting air,
even in the most obvious places.
Loudly they let.
They let with spunk
and reek of bravado.
With a taste of disdain
they let me be present to witness their let.
I think of the '60s song "Let Me"
and the '80s, this massive letting.
They let in front of Double Rainbow ice cream parlor.
They let as if there were no tomorrow
and because the trains never run on time.
They let because the moon is on its approach
or, faithless, is dashing off again.
They let because we live in permissive times
and the doors are wide open.

November 14, 1990

WHAT IS THERE TO DO TODAY?

Finland is available but hardly enough.
It's only morning, and the doctor says
Have a germ there, just might spread.
What is there to do?
I've rung up April Fishhead, forgetting she's at
work in the downtown mines.
I've washed three loads of clothes and taken
kitty on a walk, making her cross the busiest
streets in the neighborhood.
Would that I had a child to nurture!
There must be a cure.

November 14, 1990

THE PARTING
for Clint

Nightmarish, crude blond hair
tangles in too much shrubbery,
while speckled hints of boredom
enamor those garish blue eyes
that ridicule with such ease.
It's not sweetness that colors red
those strawberry cheeks.
Nor guilt, nor even blame,
and shame is gone taboo.

We both have found ourselves
adults before our time
without a stitch to our backs
or a song for our freedom
or a hope of success.
Nothing within earshot
reaches these hearts—
our drumbeats of a vast interior
that retreat into cool veins
toward dark marrow.

January 27, 1991

ADAM

Salvation comes more easily to some than to others
and then some of us are sicker than others
and may be incapable of honesty
while imagining ourselves unique.

They say last week Adam "attacked Robin Williams's baby"
which means that he was *ill-mannered* or *inappropriate*
with someone he couldn't possibly recognize as a star
as he tagged along behind Ace who's covered with jewelry
while complaining the street's become an open-air Bellevue,
referring to, of course, Adam and the attack.
Still, we must admit it's not easy
being rigorously honest and fabulous in the same day,
though when it happens, what a spiritual awakening!

When you're dying of thirst, you'll drink from a mud hole.
So we can't blame Adam for picking up the first drink
when our current crises over excess result in the penance
of sitting an hour a day on church-hall folding chairs
when one can't possibly look or feel good
flesh against metallic
and Adam is perhaps being intelligent with what is left him
when he sits on the sofa instead at the back of the room,
chomps into a big red apple
and writes furiously about something so vital
it couldn't possibly be Robin Williams
or his baby.

February 2, 1991

GOING OUT

Call for the Studebaker!
It's late, and I must flee.
The gondola mural
you've painted on the wall
has a hold on me.
I am floating down the stairs.
I am flirting with a Moorish butler.
I am reaching for cognac, thinking
what a sumptuous night to exchange
fresh skins for spice.

February 13, 1991

SOT

In a land doomed to selling postcards,
the great empire has passed its first teeter
and begun its long slide toward daily rudeness
of desperate panhandlers and those forced
to hang about street corners finagling dinner invitations,
while the solution of good citizens is
the installation of public toilets within an economy
whose toilet tissue tears anywhere
but along the intended perforation.

When the mercenary beheads the messenger,
then much like the aged pretty-boy king
is the publisher and sot Ross who once scrawled in a
black book the names of Those Who Transgressed
and now with the plague AIDS awakes each week and
shuffles in his slippers to pour over the copy editor's
sheets of his bar-rag's obituaries with joy at another
name to scratch and claw from his great black book.

February 13, 1991

FUNEREAL
for Don Sherrow

One whole ship set with an entire fire,
wasted on a dead Viking.
And now what do we get? Satin in a coffin
and a tombstone that reads "Our Beloved Son"
in English, French and German
as if you came from a tribe of translators
with aspirations toward the diplomatic corps.
Who knows which is more apropos for laying grave side
flowers of plastic or flowers of silk
when there's not only a new decade and another century
but a fresh millennium just around the corner.

There must've been a cure for the malady or lack of care
or there must be a therapy for the lack of a cure
when I don't know what to wear, beyond black, and
nothing's predictable about fashion except the lack of surprise
particularly when one leaves in a coma
without getting to brush one's teeth.
If we must have ritual,
a pyre of studio junk from the village artist
along with your university diplomas would do.

You've only yourself to blame
that you were no chief, no high priest, no war hero,
and thus we haven't supplied a ship for you
despite your suave, urbane hand in the till of civilization
and your hair cropped as if to say
I'm game, I'm game for anything.

February 13, 1991

SLIPPING INTO 20TH CENTURY
AMERICAN PAINTINGS

Because it's been a long day
I must dominate something
and the long day has dared
offend my sense of self-perfection
by requesting I toil when I should
be fed like the God I am, and thus
emotionally impaired I seek to physically harm
or physically harmed I seek to emotionally impair
though I will do both at the drop of a hat
and never say I'm sorry much less spend
a Saturday night looking desperate again.
I'll do anything to keep us together
including a murder-suicide for love
that brings notoriety, my notoriety.

March 9, 1991

NOCTURNE FOR THE NOCTURNAL
after reading The Fall *by Camus*

Through caffeine and the glow of amber traffic lights,
attempting to rest your wickedness you race
unassailable till morning, your nemesis,
when the night apparitions of magic disintegrate.

Alone, great urban centers know the sound of your boots
whose leather takes on the scent of body, your calves
as steel girders within a fond structure but moving like gods.
The city's river would reverse its trend to caress you,
could it kiss your lips with its spit in its flow through sewers
generous in spirit.

Let there be gasoline on your jeans (your heart the motor)!
The redundancies of your male side—hostile indifference—
are doomed to glorious basking in street light, no other.
But you need not be beautiful, only self-sustaining.
You could fuck yourself.
You could never descend from the castle's turret tip
till dawn's long white sheet stretches over your face.

March 9, 1991

CAFÉ HAIRDO

Well!
Special is what Special wishes, and look! Not a cryptic line
on your insipid face. I can see your whole soul down those eyes,
and you'd thought you'd sewn shut all your holes good and tight
just in time for sending your list to Santa Claus.

Well!
The hairdo is small compared to the ego that purchased it,
though you do throw fabulous parties, but, listen, you're
fooling no one pretending you open your townhouse to friends
out of generosity or love. We know your game of binding guests
thru gratitude so that as soon as something new comes to the city,
one of us, indebted, delivers it to your door that bears the trite
inscription WELCOME set by the tulips.

Well!
The Thanksgiving spread was as large as your thunderous thighs,
oh Troubadour, but after numerous desserts and too much wine
your song was more like a sick swan dying than a Pavarotti,
though the two of you do share a similar poundage and a gluttony
that benefit your respective fans.

Well!
Being tired of retail is nothing like being tired of word processing.
I drew the comparison only because who can continually be honest
in such a tired conversation when I had done everything requiring
my upkeep and, interminable, the wagging of your tongue had to
tire its organ and you also oh-so-tired in your life, aging and tired
of your longevity in selling, you'll need to get used to dates
not showing up.

                                            Well!
If it weren't for the fact I'd rather go to the gym than kill myself,
I might've returned your call. It's so banal, desiring to be fucked,
a repetition that in an earlier era embodied some aplomb.
Still, isn't leaving your sexual fantasies on answering machines
these days more desperate than the traditional lavatory walls?

                                    March 16, 1991

WHITE TRASH

You are white and trash in each corner
of an Empire as it recedes into the sunset
because your labor, though cheap, is worthless.

You are trash and blow everywhere, amassing your type
from dumps onto freeways toward junkyards, filling cars
and schools for workshops where opportunities knock.

You cost twenty bucks and lie and cheat
and have the most darling feet.

As trash you avoid the numbers of headaches that come
from tax collectors and the esteem of the merchant class,
while artists want to paint you
and poets fall in love with you,
the Irish ones especially.

July 28, 1991

BODYBUILDER

in memory of Michael Weber

Muscle kinks, infections, spider wounds
require food and rest, respite from ruffians.
Cow's milk, "tiger's milk," soy milk, carrot juice,
and high-potency brewer's yeast concentrates
presage a victory, a parading of trophies.

If I must train my body
slow on a Saturday night alone, I must.
Eventually, there's beauty in fine-tuning the chill
to personal aberration of style. Performing alone
is included in the price, a special part of the package.
I would not call the final product beautiful.
I would not limit myself to the judgments of clientele.
Reward derives from mass, but ecstasy thrives on process.
All that's required is survival
after mucking through the warmth of Mother, terrible
childhood, the first young fucks and mistook loves,
the absorption of knowledge that didn't quite cut bait,
as fishermen say, and it is a little like fishing,
years of never making muscle, then presto—
a powerhouse of loneliness!
A professional in muscular docility!

Now, those with the infamous venom
are small nuisance to me in any bed, on any beach.

August 23, 1991

BED MAKING

Blood on white carpet! will never come out.
It must be from spite, this disparagement.
The character's revealed, smoking after each kill.
Then there's the compulsion to conversation
when no one's listening,
invariably too much self-revelation in darkness.

Nothing's incessant but lust with so many
beautiful young lollipops and white-meat thighs.
This skinny breast has a secret odor that banks
on insecurity, creating an astounding magic.
A good Christian takes to all of humanity
as brethren, then changes the sheets.

December 1, 1991

ENVY

My friend Chuck, you spend your energies
envying the lover of beautiful blond Dane.
In your loneliness, you dwell on what you lack.

Count your blessings when alone in your room.
Your illusion's better than their truth.
That Dane is incapable of faithfulness.

His lover owns the pain of knowing
what he possesses tonight
is second or even third hand.

January 31, 1992

AFTER HIS DEATH

Words like lesion, bile, pneumocystis
have battled and won over your tongue.
From a gingerbread Victorian, you watch
fog cancel the San Francisco dream,
think of the one hundred bowls of gruel
you spoon fed him with "Eat!,"
think of his books decaying in the basement
shipped from Madison or Ann Arbor,
think of lovers in this city
who retreat down slim alleys marked
NOT A THROUGH STREET,
ending it with a hoarse whisper
and leaving you two cats.
One Siamese.
One a skewed version.

Tonight you put on your best leather,
go out in a mantle of masculinity.
You only know old habits.
Who can say they're bad ones?

February 16, 1992

CLUB URANUS

All the dogs of Europe bark
– W.H. Auden, "In Memory of W.B. Yeats"

It's a dog-eat-dog world that's full of clubs
$10 to get in, and all the dogs
which means the entire species
travel now in packs
hounds tie bandannas round sagging necks
coyotes buckle silver above crooked tails
old wolves smolder in leather
and sly young foxes preview naiveté in shorts
   when not the season
this is called *going out*

The yelping starts at 12
by hyenas exiled from back-street Phoenix
who maybe get to say "I'm from Calgary"
when dropped by Greyhounds in San Francisco
it's hysterical
this activity they call *laughing*

Some purr like cats with tongues withdrawn
having waxed their winter fur
by the fire by couple but still
dogs, stupid and vacant-eyed,
this they call *the look of love*

The remainder scatter across the floor
circling in pursuit of their own tails
this act they believe attractive
aping anarchy by defying form

y tambien casi sin la ropa
"and also almost without clothing"
their bones buried beneath stone
they call this *dancing*

No one dares stay outside these days
that would require a skill in language
        and all the pretense, the posing,
        is for the herd, within the herd, and herd
        versus herd, *Oh Europe in the desert*
        of America, a steady gale forbids more
        than greasing the conduction of commerce
        and engagement in sacred rites of trade
these, all the dogs perform
these skills, all dogs have

May 2, 1992

ACT OF GOD
for Sam Baird

Gosh, I feel like Lazarus emerging from the tomb
albeit minus Jesus who's busy ticketing parking meters
and chastising groups of orange pickers who lack smog checks.

It's tit for tat to grasp reality at this late date
when I've dusted off years in just two months
and can't recall scoring!

Despite the horrid scars, someone gorgeous might love
my inner child or my outer style, or so says Mary.

There's balance in imbalance. Half of beauty consists of
a catchy walk and sincere smile. Besides, I've a new complexion
after so much cortisone my skin's tight as smooth bone.

Drawing out objects of love is spiritually shrewd.
Inflate them in conversations in drawing rooms.
Discussing oneself bores everyone when everyone's obsessed
with oneself but lonely and so converses in the first place.
It's all a chore and less than uplifting.

Would I could afford to be either decadent or bourgeois.
That I'm oriented toward improvement is my salvation.
Too late for tennis, place me between wickets in cricket
and I'll hit hither and thither, whatever is there!

May 18, 1992

VANITY

I've a knack for attracting the supercritical like flies.
Roommates, for example, who tell me I'm too
self-conscious or I just lack confidence,
as if one's interchangeable with the other,
that I should be dating
or I'm too vain if I need access to the bathroom
for a look in the mirror before going out
even though I don't date
and if I'm that vain
I should spring for a mirror in my own room.
"Need the mirror!?!" they shout at my knock.
Or they amuse themselves with the finding of flaws,
as if given license by past transgressions like
last year's raspberry cheesecake never replaced.
"So when did you get your nose broken?" asks one.
The other says I've got spare tires around my waist.
"Still going to the gym?" Implying I'm not vain enough.

In the end, for two hundred dollars
I buy a vanity mirror and have it inscribed
Resentment is the Potting Soil of Scars.
And move. I was just cheap.

May 24, 1992

BRUTALLY HONEST

Afflicted with some odd presumptions
you summon me over the phone,
which makes for an edgy evening, to begin with.
Did a lousy oracle lead you astray
or so many movies you started living them?
I mean I'm a man and with some taste
yet I'm supposed to drop a monogrammed hanky
along Fifth Avenue for you to pick up
like I'm some silky '50s starlet.

Honestly, must I point out the obvious?
That you resemble Godzilla—
the American version—
when the pasty makeup job indicates
you'd looked into the mirror
and seen something in need of subterfuge.
And your fangs! as with horses
the teeth are a dependable indicator
of a disease that's begun to unmask itself.

June 13, 1992

FEMALE DREAMS

I.

I'm in my mother's kitchen in this dream.
I'm a grown woman and this confuses me
because Mom still looks 30, her hair teased
and not gone gray.
She spanks me while I dry the dishes.
The dream ends when I break one.

II.

I ride a streetcar that stops at a boulder in the tracks
separating city from field, skimping on the suburbs.
I'm thinking, "This is symbolism!"
I'm the only passenger who's stayed on.
The conductor says, "End of the line, lady."
Next, I'm milking a cow with my heels kicked off.
It's hilly and green. I note
when I sweat, my body cools.
CUT TO: I'm in a hot field in a flat land.
The cow is gone. I'm in an old dress and
Panama hat. My back aches from picking strawberries.
I hear myself saying, "If they're organic
I'll *never* get them cleaned in time for dessert."

III.

I'm in an old town with narrow streets.
Must be Europe. My stomach hurts.
Would anyone do anything should I faint?
It's a late twilight, between shadows

when light belongs to stone.
A cat crosses my path and freezes.
Holding straw from my broom like the whiskers
of a mouse in my fist, I woo her.
"Here kitty kitty, nice kitty."
Curious, she comes for the killing.
I grab her by the neck and twist.
Screams always draw a crowd.
You can smell the children, sweet but dirty.
"Oooh, DIN-ner," says a little girl.

IV.

This is the dream I don't wake up from.
I lie on a stretcher next to a van.
A cop pulls the sheet over my face.
She's a woman. I'm thinking,
if I'm dead, how can I smell her,
a blend of sweat and perfume?
FADE OUT

December 24, 1992

LIKE THE CLAP OR SOME CHRONIC DISEASE

White skin, its upbringing, that fetish with puss.
And always just off-beat—the noise you make's more
harmful than the smell of your feet.
Nothing's innocuous that appears to be. Recall how
those nasty Communists would clap in unison at Party Congresses.
Fortunately, torpedoes for the torpid disturb a generic passivity
determined by the philosophical ramifications of fresh fruits
versus vegetables. So, where's the action?
All of it with the turgid ones shopping incessantly
and so enthusiastically nothing else has any import—
we only acted like it did before, in cafés, in marches,
                              under the sheets, if you will—
while imports are the rage these days, constituting the craze
                              not just for blonds, the Euro thing,
but how much possessed in addition to from whence
and what brand, when everything's said to be in a name.
If I just had a picture of it! Oh, Holy Name!
All our gurus returned to India packing penicillin.
It's best to go along in life, worry about death later.

Fireworks induce parties toward gaiety, the splendid,
when idolizing the host was the intention.
I entertain by reciting all the social diseases in Latin
before escaping into taxis committing us from club to club and
the blurry hazards of falling in love surrounded by mirrors—
our souls stuck again in wardrobe and no coat check.

"Being Christian," "a Christian being,"
"especially a Christian," "even a Christian,"
can't imagine the transgressions I've forgiven
in songs of masturbation after Dusty Springfield's

"I Just Don't Know What To Do With Myself"
off vinyl and onto CD, miracles of the program
a kind of pogrom, a healthy little social purge.
As I could not be Orthodox, my icons evolve
from acts of consumption—blood for goods
and the exchange of body fluids.
In reality, the language could kill us.
Never mind the AIDSpeak that creeps in.
Similar self-destructions led to monasteries during plague.
And I've figured it out.
You mean as much to my life as the World Bank, more
than the World Court but less than the World Woo Woo.
The smell of that leg after 49, a malodorous wickedness
like a vanished epidemic I've just begun to miss.
I'd rather sit under a tree and watch the apples drop
than have another kiss, thank you.

February 12, 1993

THE LOST CHILD

in memory of Dean Reeves

There's beauty sometimes in getting lost, a serene moment
while descending the stairs after a bath, unwrapping the towel,
and presto! You hear music, a little symphony, maybe even your choice.
For some, it's Gary Puckett and the Union Gap's "Woman, Woman."
For others, it might be the Dixie Cups, something innocuous
while arranging flowers in an olive-green vase on a translucent day
before smacking the brat across the room, toward the wall
with the Van Gogh print of "Still Life and a Vase."

Or it's a good book.
Or, better, a best-selling book about serial killers or "film stars,"
the kind you can really eat up.
When a child, reading in a closet can be beneficial to the mind
                                        if the lighting's good.

                                        February 27, 1993

REWARD FOR SHOWING UP

Long the farthing of my eye,
there you are, useful as a Los Angeles suburb
displaying a fasces of sticks with protruding blade
intended as a symbol of authority.
Or just phallic. But still a boundary, a mark.

Socially, this lifetime seems defined by
whom we meet in sudatoriums, all that leisure
while separating one's needs defined by body
from one's needs defined by mind.
The histamine versus antihistamine, if you will.
An age-old conflict.

Once upon a time, we branded slaves.
Now slaves wear brand names
awing in consumption, one would wager.
See the cancerous transfixed by their lesions.
This is beautiful, rubbing on moisturizers. Development
implies a romanticism that makes buying potatoes sexy.

Maybe I'm looking for an aberration, a freak of nature,
staying up till 4 for a good song.
Not enough imagination in forming our lives
implies we wallow in history, of which we're also ignorant.
Oh, take me home. You're dumb and homely but still warm,
unique in every way.

March 14, 1993

THE ACQUISITION OF NOTHING

Club discounts among tempting summer sales!
When opportunity knocks, my palms open
ready to be nailed.
For fun I name the social interactions around me—
Pretty Obtuse Clawing the Thin Skin of Hercules, for example.

Not all interactions enhance commerce, explicitly,
even while perfecting self improvements called *professional*.
I indulge myself in weaknesses morose and idiomatic,
insubstantial and of no consequence except
                                    they hold me back.

I'm told there are women more aggressive.

It's not easy to propel one's spirit through this
nocturnal society ruled by the hard wit of seminary dropouts
                                    cutting for advantage.

My worst fear blooms:
Being Spoken To, when and where I might choose, finding
words too few to waste on those obsessed
by the inherent value of what is gained.
Or what would be gained by a hostage taken
                                    into the night.

Or being a hostage taken in the night. Rather,
I'll be the first to leave, rushed by the thrill of loss,
due to the Irish in me or the pagan antipathy.

Serious eye contact only flirts with sincerity.
Intrigue fails to import itself into a shotgun head

with the bold stare and everlasting hair over there.
Even the prettiest of pictures appears grotesque,
with discussions about *strength* indicating a rote blindness
when showing off was the intention.

I'm wearing a mask tonight that's thirty-five years old.
It's not been easy. Like a tree,
I've grown thirty-five rings around me,
a willow in a droopy state, my best young oak
with a poker face, a cedar now improving its posture,
the real bully bathing in purity, underneath.
These seeds we cultivate, these we feed the starving.
And the music?
Ninnies consumed!

May 5, 1993

A SOCIAL CREATURE

If I were to visit, often, that notorious place better not named
I too might care for its sort of itching—
fetishism, elongations, and hairy octagonal backs.
But, too soon, I feel the yawns coming on.

I believe taste a child of environment.
Most haven't enough of either, which I call poverty
over my therapist's virulent objections.
Judgmental again! Be tolerant, open to anything
and never discriminating. That *egalite-liberte* vein
called modernism that pushed libraries.

The rest of us, kids in a candy store,
what the "working" class call *spoiled* or *brat*,
theoretically Jamesian, free for intellectual pursuits,
are essentially nincompoops lonely at the core.
Jealousy effects the pussy, envy the purse.
Get it straight. Failure to separate the two
leaves one muddled and confused, and it's a long life.

Don't be arch, you might become aloof
when really you desired to lick a Nazi's boot,
an endeavor in revival today as "safe" sex.
Unleash yourself to slavery and health!
Arbeit macht frei, and the air is good.

Any behavior's a function of class in a classless society
of therapists upset and theologians passé,
and everyone says, "*I* am middle class"
like the sound of (sigh) the unspoken whisper
"Am I too *big* for you?" From excess of experience

in the boudoir, so to speak, these analogies gush
us back into futile circles of buying and selling
when—sorry—I preferred the curves of love.
Oh misery! Born into the wrong age again
with alterations to the atmosphere no remedy.

May 15, 1993

LITANY ON A PERFECT ASS

My disdain for acknowledging the two small nights
of your generous body
was not intended to belittle
the perfection of its constructed virtues so contained.
Let me explain.

Too soon the usual complications set in:
adolescent tastes in film
I attribute to a lack of instruction
and a preference for the biggest
pop stars with the least talent
I attribute to a working-class aversion to irony
and the painless opinions on issues of the day
I attribute to never developing an ideology
and growing up in a fledgling society
I attribute to not wanting to think
and the lack of reaction to my vocation
I attribute to never reading
and your fears of aging and balding
I associate with the most banal of brethren
and imagining yourself skinny
I attribute to a genetic fear of famine.

All of this in an age as terrifying in truth
as my age in contrast to your youth—
its disclosure always a mistake
despite which you come off heroic
if, or because, not absolutely pliable.
What balls!
As if by leaving the lights on you can sell more insurance.

The significance of those two nights reveals itself
in your intrigue with size—so American—
the one real compliment, the full circle
of physical attributes once meant to complete each other.

May 31, 1993

RIVALRY

I want to know who my rivals are. Which of the young men who
decline in this café licking cigarettes through fast, caffeine *adieu*'s
invoke their sorceries muffled between your thighs?
I want the names of these anonymous gods you fail to fear.
I want a full listing of their self-images,
of what-sort upbringings that come after birth. All
that captivates you beyond just another pretty face.
The schools, the divisions, the allegiances to whom.
I must have a recipe, a means of competition,
a forthright enterprise for exploitation so I might fix my failure.
I want your perceptions of perfection in the bodies of my rivals,
the flesh you won't let go of despite your loud spirituality worn
as a smart smock that's vintage but sexy, not too tattered
and always stylish.

As for your "pieces," they're good, a stream of goodness like all
you emulate. In an era of ceaseless absorption, you are tireless.
Maybe it's you who gets easily assimilated into global consciousness
with the agility you show in slipping between so many sheets.
Maybe it's you who wins the prize of annihilation and I join
my former rivals scouting the plains for fresh meat
or a place to sleep. And there you are, like a mirage—
photographed for the papers, bald in Stockholm,
pinnacle of civilization at the top of your shiny head.

Still, what is the common thread not so elegant,
the black line you pull while extracting the guts?

May 31, 1993

EASTER 1981

Sowing seeds of miracles, the winter rains abruptly cease.
I voyage home through slick, cobblestone streets
from the cathedral, redeemed, the click of my heels,
the din of bells echoing, delirious.
The radio's reasonable voice:
Ronald Reagan wishes Happy Easter,
a Significantly Diminished Passover.
I think of long freight trains that circumvent the city,
    a boxcar with my name on it,
    work that soon will set me free.
I think of Reagan together with Peron or even Petain,
    the Grand Marshall who traded the largest army in Europe
    for a corner on the Vichy water market.
All the old pigs go to market eventually.
It's an obligatory orgy before death.
Certain aspects of their copulation come to mind,
the folds of flesh, the fatty breasts, the stench of the unclean.

It's spring, and I'm new in this patriotic skin
    tight from gelatin additives, tight as youth.
Emerging from a cave, I'm a medieval hermit with a fresh bouquet
    thanks to national-chain florists advertising Mercurial speed,
    emerging with Weimar chocolates, assorted and crème-filled.
An American Social Revolutionary with neither American Dream
    nor peasants to liberate from so-called nobility,
    I'm like dashing Kerensky invited by the Bolsheviks
    to leave in 1917, barhopping Manhattan throughout
    the twenties, thirties, forties, fifties,
    and sixties until dashed, finally dashed but
    the hair well-matted and perfumed, a French pomade.
A citizen but not really a member, I could end up with an ice pick

through my skull, assassinated down in Mexico.
I'm a near visitor, uninvited but strange to no one,
    a mule, a freak, a doll, I'm like a cockroach,
    pre-Christian and never completely removed.

I'm a goat breeding "goatinos" in Arkansas.
I'm a well-bred, well-endowed lunatic whoring toward Washington.
I'm engaged to commerce, and any opening is my pussy
        where high-pitched screams of despair are the common law.
I'm a post-op manufacturer of soup lines staffed by smiling volunteers.
I could well be the cause, their bane of existence, a favorite charity.
I'm on an all-expense-paid Caribbean cruise, gratuities included.
Through the porthole I wave at romance from a point of expertise
        and no matter how murky the vision, I still see.
I'm a refugee with a suitcase full of worthless Vichy currency
        and redemptive papers due to clerical error.
For kicks, I'm in bunny ears,
        a midget prostitute giving head at the St. Moritz bar
        to James Dickey and Ginger Rogers, dancing.

On window sills sit bowls of painted eggs
blown till hollow shell, dusty with the years,
reminders of the day. And the case?
Closed long ago.

                                        May 31, 1993

IMPORT, EXPORT

Up late with loneliness and the invitations go out
for more bondage with a stranger, another bad fit.

The bravest of both the natives and the exiled living here—
the ardent, the preying-but-delightful—
tired of the bars and sex standing up, with nothing else new
for diversion, sometimes peep through youth hostel windows
at European faces absorbing baseball scores
and look for difference beyond language.

Chuck says, at the beach they're arrogant
when it comes to sex, which translates as
"when in Rome do as the Romans" when sweetness
or generosity might better meet all our needs.
We don't ask for much from the Germans who come
and rent Buicks from Alamo here.
An occasional surprise, a frequent spontaneity,
a birthday remembrance, a profound lust would be too much.
Viewed from behind the tinted glass of touring cars or
over thrown-back convertibles, we are the strangers,
the gays even, our awful feelings picked at
and mocked, near suicides in fond but simple terms.
Now the darlings of our various, respective chambers of commerce.
As sophisticates in matters of theater, a perfect find
in its adopted habitat! Voting, tax-paying, well-adjusted.
                                                            So,
no, I can't fathom going back to Rome from my little bundle
of beaver sticks, my racket of variations on nadir themes.
The plummeting dollar would make a shattering fall
of wheelbarrowing up to the counter to pay for fast food.
I might have to look at myself!

Nothing's enjoyable if not throwing money around,
that most cross-cultural activity of the bourgeoisie.
Saturday nights alone are better borne near home
with something to look at like architecture—
these Victorians, these bay windows,
the TransAmerica pyramid and the Marriott we call The Jukebox—
and the assurance of preserving one's youth
with a jar of optimism, on hold for future use.

As part of its continuous promotion, we must live with
overproduced music meant for foreign consumption,
the kind you just dance to since it can't be spoken over,
as perfect as intentions can be—a good fit.
"This is a nice place."

                              Just dancing
                              evokes a net
which ends anything but a pantomime.

Even the pretty get blocked. The pores clog.
Think of Big Mama patting the bed Liz Taylor and Paul Newman
no longer share in *Cat on a Hot Tin Roof*
with her "it's all made here" gesture to Liz.
Or what Chuck calls "disappointing ass."
When you pull the pants down, you're free
for nothing, available for emptiness.
Shopping for groceries might evoke similar feelings.
You squeeze soggy New Zealand melons and,
for some sort of fruit, settle for California prunes.

                                        June 6, 1993

CALIGULA OR NIXON LEAVING

Embarking on withdrawal mandated by the Senate,
in a cold sweat he ascends the stairs of departure
and turns to face a stunned mob and habitually
sticking out his arms, an addict for the last hit,
he waves generously, a ridiculous gesture, really he flails,
and drags his starved and forever-blonde empress
into the Department of War helicopter
after violating his daughter,
who's in tears, married to respectability,
and absolutely, beyond question,
it's a new era, though a crisis in government
we must all survive less the million dollars he took.
What's done is done, the incoming empress looking like
Grace Jones on downers singing "Warm Leatherette,"
and as the helicopter lifts from the Rose Garden lawn
from some place like Istria or Capri and a fat bank branch,
three guards roll up the red carpet
as if we'd never invited him into the palace
in the first place.

June 23, 1993

SALÒ AT THE CASTRO
for Kurt

David has the better parts on tape.
Peter's seen it once at the Strand—the *old* Strand
before the switch to Schwarzenegger posings and serial killings.
Victory to the brute forces of nature, once again.
Ah, the class struggle when the masses win,
and the prize still smells of stale urine!

Now *Salò* arrives uptown—at the Castro—for "A Pasolini
Retrospective" with searchlights the first night along a street
customized by post-radical lesbians who now wear makeup
and move sweetly in line, past teeming ice-cream and cookie shops
and the boys down from Twin Peaks and too much spite
searching for their inner child in the gay chain bookstore
or who walk matching Pekinese past. And, appropriately,
a retrospective that closes with this *Salò*, this controversial
gem, the poet-filmmaker's final reel before murder, shown in
a neighborhood whose men are mostly dead or about to be.
Summer stock keeps the flies away.
We know all the tricks of show biz—it's innate!
A twist of genetics all along, the studies say.
Thank you, Goddess, and bless you, Science!
Those queens on Castro hardly know who Mussolini is,
and if you mention the Second Empire,
they think you mean furniture.
Interior decorators and hairdressers, yes, but scratch
and you get loan officers and salesmen and "non-profit" cheats
who promenade with wishy-eyed models along Castro Street.
The prosperous proletariat anxious to pump itself
into the bourgeois logjam of more upon more.

Kurt, a blue-collar punk, wouldn't go to the Castro
and wouldn't know the film either. Rather,

he lives it, works two days a week in The City,
dwells in the more-affordable Mountain View,
says nothing goes on down there.
Occurrence takes some distance to appreciate.
From the gut—someone's or anyone's—his mouth stays full.
Tangibly, to be consumed!
I want my shit eaten too!

August 5, 1993

CHRISTMAS PARTY ABOVE THE CASTRO

It's like flying, nervous and not wanting to go.
From the beginning, afraid opportunity won't knock.
With hands open like a priest's over the spit,
the host receives me, unknown nondescript soul.

There was Bernard, interior,
sporting a sort of bob, exterior.
That hairdresser needs axe murdering.
These spiritual excretions that just don't look good.
A big clone in leather passing out gin.
And some little twinkie just passing out.
They take an acquired taste.
Never too late for parties,
never too early for fashion,
I order apple juice in a wine glass.
It helps me mingle among the avant-garde.

"Most Favorite" goes to the blond in the marine dress
uniform, a smile that's frosting on the cake. I mean,
he seems friendly! Is there acid in the juice?
Some guy whispers, "He's tweaked."
A spoiler finds the wound and barrels in,
driving off the competition. Opinion appears
not unanimous in this—this icon, this marine I want
to ask *are you real*? I don't even like blonds, I think.
David says he's darling, is as much interested in the dip
which is appropriate at 50, wants to talk about Yaddo.
I say I thought he dressed a lot, which is too much.
A cadet would better do, they still read, he sighs.
No one cute can talk, it would wreck a perfect picture
even in my neighborhood, part of the city.
The roaming clown reminds me of drag queens, missing
or forbidden—bottoms to a high mortality rate?

Then two arrive, psychic, somewhat subdued.
With champagne flowing from a fountain
this could be Baton Rouge. But the end involves
leaving with the coat-check guy in all those muscles.
He puts on a yellow leather jacket.
Yellow. We go downhill from there.

September 5, 1993

DATABASE TERMINUS

For a piece of cheesecake, most of us concert with the regime
going along for the getting along. Genetic makeup
can create a big to-do as well as a hell of a rig-a-ma-roll.
You'll never get back out once you've thrown yourself into it.
There's no retrieval process possible See Manuel [sic]
when the action is all about feeling, beyond the stomach.
Then breeding to boot duplicates the stupidity as
accomplishment in frying fish over an open fire.

Each generation needs a goddess for instruction in techniques.
Sometimes it's just knowing the process of which pile to pull from.
Or is that "file to put to" or "window to pull down"?
If I don't get the flow of response soon, I'll have a crash
on my hands or an electrocution and fail to speak or move.
Such disabling could clog processing or, worse, stop the waltz.

Luckily, a glorious few are meant for managing emergencies,
waking to their fortes during earthquakes, major fires, or holocausts.
Control is a disease of loss spread through power outages.
Happily, bonding to a carrier implies freedom from indemnity.
Any application that fails to anoint complexity encourages sin.
"Even the homeless are merry!" observed Yeltsin on a visit in.
Besides, in a barbecue democracy, we've elected our security.
We've certainly had our say.

September 10, 1993

JINX

I'd sooner kill myself than go to that bar
regardless of your fabulous haircut
and your hunch that this is your lucky night
after innumerable lousy ones and after
I've been good enough to you for years
or better than most. In fate, what you get
is doubtlessly what you deserve.
I don't blame you for wanting to break the spell
tonight and step out in a new mask:
pumped into a gel of optimism.
Life's a delirium of variability with billions
in the world, and so it's difficult to explain
why yours always comes up zero.

September 15, 1993

BOYFRIEND X ARTISTE

Spoiling in fresh air, that sharp artistic temperament
becomes a filament in tempera, mounted and glassed
in a gallery that made room for you and then closed
despite commendations from the *Daily Nonsense*
on the baring of your soul, unseen in looking up your ass.

From the cool opening to the closing farewell,
was it more like a requiem or just another screw?
There's a lot around town lately, flaws in scheduling,
these embarrassments from too much success,
these numerous pieces rich with agrarian wholesomeness.

As for my withdrawal, more from the shallow salesman's
cheap pitch than the stroke of your rampant, unrelenting appetite
so notorious and trite in our little corner of the world.

                                        October 25, 1993

FEMALE IMPERSONATOR

for Sean Penn

There must be a formula in the cosmos, in the abstract.
Something that sticks and stays stuck.
Something marketable but lasting.
Something that keeps men hot.

Like magic, like an answered prayer, along comes MacDonna
like a little girl produced to slut. Inevitably
like a teenage abortion after a long rough night,
the overdubs echo in vast chambers
in the wake of sound engineers, the real butchers,
the professionals. Out comes
one is such a lonely number, aah, aah, aah
in addiction to twenty-six times
open your heart, I'll make you love me
lines MacDonna wrote herself
from her own life experience, we're told.
The complexities. It must have been tragic.

When movies need miracles to still make millions,
clips of MacDonna ascend from cutting-room floors
and meld into cameos and a chunk of the gross.
The "new Marilyn Monroe"? Makeup! Cocaine!

October 26, 1993

HANGOVER

Fetal days curled up in bed and calling in,
and it *is* like being sick
jammed back up the womb
with pieces slow to fit the fast night of it.

Evidence crawls from under the blackout:
peep show tokens among spare change
                    in addition to
a last request on The Stud's notepaper—
"please let me fuck you"
                              over
a drawing of a drooling dick.
The third and best installment is
branded on flesh nearest the heart,
a ring of care that circles my left tit
with teeth marks in the bruise of it,
sore from love
or sick from its lack.

November 13, 1993

YOU REMIND ME A LITTLE OF NAPOLEON

Because it's been a long day
I must dominate something
and the long day has dared
offend my sense of self-perfection
by requesting my toiling when I should
be fed like the God I am, and thus
emotionally impaired I seek to physically harm
or physically harmed I seek to emotionally impair
though I will do both at the drop of a hat
and never say I'm sorry much less spend
a Saturday night looking desperate again.
I'd do anything to keep us together
including a murder-suicide like a Hapsburg heir
who couldn't wait thirty years.

You are even more stunning than the one in February
I stalked through 20th Century American paintings.
So stunning, this time I must muster my assertiveness
without sinking into the usual ambiguities.
History's great lesson—action over talk!
I imagine myself clubbing you, dragging you off
by the hair to my basement cave, watching you sleep
while I love and whisper "I do, I do" and come
and have basket-loads of cocker spaniels
in lieu of children in bassinets with whom to sublimely
affirm the bliss of going through
apartment shuffling, furniture upgrades, career moves
and coloring our hair the identical tint like twins
because this or that is my whim
and throwing you across a room
when I'm in the mood after you hurt my pride

by requesting I clip my toenails
because they scratch you in bed
and cracking your shin to see if it hurts
then kissing it to make it well and never
spending a Saturday night alone again
or, worse, spending one looking and looking desperate
and at the successful conclusion of the first five-year plan
whispering in your ear
I'd do anything to keep us together
which of course includes a murder-suicide
making all the worst papers
notoriety, any notoriety
better than the finest painting
nothing cuter in 20th century rooms.

November 13, 1993

THE STEAM ROOM

Invasions by amphibians and reptiles signal the end
of lap swim. With Roman grins, the snakes slither in
                                    from the peristyle pool
after forcing the newts out the fast lane.
The goggled and swim-capped pointy heads of salamanders
survey the empire by the steam-room door,
apprentices toward professional one-upsmanship.
Occupation without exercise—a paradise!
And here come the frogs! An old toad plops itself above
the bloated dinosaur fossilizing in marble but
who speaks! And to the lone, lost chicken he says
"So what are *you* doing Valentine's Day?"

Pockmarked crocodilians thrive on Pollyanna looks.
Starving India's poor cousin to the alligator,
the gavial, have the sharpest teeth but thinnest beak
for breaking bones, another evolutionary mystery. All varieties
of lizard fete and, with forked tongues slipping in and out,
invoke ancient arousals as the steam cycle turns on.
The Permian Period, when glaciers moved south.
Here the iguana's night lasts eternally in subdued hisses.
And those legless, wormy lizards too have names.
Oh, San Francisco, I love you for being
so cosmopolitan even the caecilians visit your Y's!

                                    January 8, 1994

THE TREES ARE WRONG: A NATURE POEM

Still more foliage cluttering up a lovely skyline!
This constant weeding, this undeserved punishment after centuries
of employing land-clearing slaves and pioneers followed by convicts
to finish the job—between arts and crafts—hacking to the ground
each bush pompadour, each affected shrub.

The trees are wrong, hardly an institution capable of producing
a marketable sound in sound studies. And still spreading!
This fertility indicates our impotence regarding wrong.
It's a crime, *like* crime, as *with* crime.
Everyone says what everyone says until several crises evolve—
the failure of Wonder calcium breads to build a strong family
and not enough cosmetics for even a low-key survival or wondering
whether the *aqua fresca* at the taqueria has too much sugar in it.
I have to know.
I have to have these "I have" issues no one else gives a damn about.
When there's too much to absorb in so little time and pandemonium
breaks out at Saks, who's got time to read the manual?
Likewise with sex partners, bodies numbed by success lose recall.
In a gentle tumble, it all comes down splendidly
and sits by God, a smiling wreck.

June 5, 1994

WHY I DON'T LIVE THERE

My friend Anthony, with your six days of recovery,
you have trouble fathoming someone like me
who prefers keeping a distance of at least
one mile from that notorious street. I'm not unique.
Some of us don't care for its associations, the "oh
girl" presumptions, the delusions of significance.
I don't dislike or disapprove. Everyone loves
a clown and clowning around, and some even love.
But theater on the street gets tiresome as the
continual ebb of one's history for the sake of the group.
The individual and the collective shouldn't be opposed,
yet I lose myself in conforming to these so-called
non-conformists—it's like Communists throwing a party!
So you're astonished I'd rather sleep in my own bed
in my own neighborhood, away from the rut of this
month's trendy club, butch and fem, tops and bottoms,
experts in discomfort which line that street.
That I live in a district halfway across the City
should tell you something, not that I can't afford
a place there. But, no, this is once again
the seventh day of your recovery. Get some rest
before resuming your obsession with men and bars.
Another week's routine of looking to be [seen] [scene]
could break that camel's back of yours.

                                        June 5, 1994

CLUB EXILE

for Matt

Here in greenhouses and arboretums
egos and tulips grow huge. Soon after the transplant
come the hormones and their steroid cousins
up from Hollywood for the hardwood floors
and Victorian backdrop, attempting to act.
A city of parks even God likes to visit,
corralling the few trees with the remaining buffalo,
each making up for the other's lack,
a most cosmopolitan dot on the map
with every cuisine from A to Z
and the country's best-read labor pool.
The city foreigners most want to see, we're told.

But where the gulls circle.
If they only knew our little Napoleon
under the ring of Canary Island palms.
If only the tourists and the fresh ones
shuttling into town could be forewarned.

June 5, 1994

SKIPPY

for Mark Mischke

He's a twinkie 20-something and comes from
what everybody's calling Generation X
which is something like a brand-name credence
suffering from what Bush called "the vision thing."
Issues around lack, very American.

All along upper Market Street they skip here,
back and forth   from A-T-M

         up and down

to bar to shop to café to sham of gym
(muscles now considered tired—at last
the pendulum has swung whisking thin back in!).
Some of them still roll on skateboards
but more and more just skip along. Little
goes on, except as slaves to fashion.
Work's such a bore, Skippies get real pagan.
They all do That Look and come in gobs.

                         July 19, 1994

GARDEN PARTY

to Patrick Sweeney, for Rick Nelson

We're all Bozos on this bus waiting for the electrician
or someone like him. I'm not mechanical
which tends to imply
I'm electric! like I should be someone
if I'm not doing something. Or is that some *one*?
There are no coincidences.
It must be difficult being homeless
and vegetarian. Does anyone drive here?
I have a perfect record and a renewal but nothing
to spend next month in Amsterdam. Just trying
to make conversation. There must be a medication
for that. Cycling's good for the butt,
the heart as well. I'm afraid of someone
dropping LSD in my tea or a lousy halibut
entering into the stew. The perfect host preselects
the orgy room with proviso of an abundance
of fluffy pillows for the chosen few
learning to socialize by the tulips
without alcohol. Chuck says they're all radical fairies,
fuck like rabbits. If I could just find someone
to pay the phone bill. You looked perfect.
That low self-esteem smoking in the sun.
There are no accidents, only interventions.
So don't let a little *déjà vu* frighten you.
I think I've got some of it on tape.
The Maintenance of Spontaneity
                    coming after
The Stiff Upper Lip.
Say, I'll bet you're a tit man.
Who invited that Philistine, anyway?

November 2, 1994

VANCE MUST DIE

Another tedious flirtation rotted out.
Youth's wasted on the young, my father'd say, but especially
these days. You've accepted my calling card endlessly,
but raise the phone and this spell's magic would cease.
The proliferation of pagan beliefs we're witnessing!
Or, it's just all about fear and the use of instruments
while appearing fashionable. Scratch and it comes off.
Your type eagerly insulates itself with The Flirt.
As Gorgeous himself once said, "Assholes protect themselves."
And he should know.

Oh, you'll probably live forever working in cafés
and "performing art" while your charm lasts, but without
a dental plan the teeth go quick and you'll come out
toothless shuffling in slippers through the French Quarter
and from the development of bad habits
negotiating your elephant thighs into an ungrateful sauna.

Optimistic, you sprout April pigtails
for a June landing at the mouth of the Hudson.
Should New York take note of its renaissance
with dancing in the Village and "a piece" in the *Voice*?
D-day with you at the heart of it, cold-eyed and bushy-tailed,
God's gift to our liberation. Oh let's have you hit
by a cab in a crosswalk for assuming the light
turning green meant it safe.

November 2, 1994

I AM TO MEET A DANE

I am to meet a Dane,
a friend informs me.
I possess an introduction,
a phone number, a bag of grass.
I am to meet a Dane,
cute, blond, pliable.
Now when I look out my window
I wave to any blind passerby,
"I am to meet a Dane!"

December 4, 1994

MY ALMA MATER HONORS A WHORE
OF THE REPUBLIC

Elizabeth Dole at Emory

Belaud! Belaud!
There's no cost for praises,
so we're enthusiastically denying the dying millions nothing.
This is the throne an Emperor Bonzo comes to.
I'm tired of blue hair and Anarchist black in the back of Cadillacs
when there's not been a meaningful suicide since Elvis
and we used to have them all the time
which certainly does not mean Wonderful Wednesdays at our college
back in the nineteen seventies were better than Tight-Fist Tuesdays
or the now-raging Throwback Thursdays. Let's be clear
we were never made happy by the whole world smiling together
while a bottle of soda sings from a hilltop
nor by the upward tick of Coca-Cola stock.

And this, this cold-tit whore you present in ridiculous pumps
as some sort of liberal is far away your worst assault on truth.
Your lauding of each other is as loud as the caw of the rare egret
desperate for attention.
Who wants her after so many Presidents each had her three ways?

January 21, 1995

BOUNDARY

for George

Antithesis of rebel, the bad apple's no black sheep
which can be identified and then expelled.
It rots too near the core.
Are there no institutions for the innocuous
unable to contribute to the common good?
Perhaps he's the one who says the stupidest things
and you wonder, conscious deceit or a true ignoramus?
Know your boundaries and stand firm in saying no.
Identification is crucial but elusive west of the Dnieper.
Hanging laundry out to dry risks overexposure.
An intimate turns you in to the authorities, anonymously.
The state plays accuser, arbiter, and judge, all in one.
It owns the body commanded from its breeders—yours.

There's no law against the law when distrust is ultimate power.
Your underwear has the wrong inseam, your unpressed shirts
do not impress. The Church has handed over its realm;
no one of us knows if this was unwilling or a deal was struck.
We are not involved except as servants,
although, of course, our betrayal remains.
But this is hypothesis and easily denied as obvious.
"Everything's in deniability," says the vice president
just prior to his promotion. But the green cat
next to the vase through the window watching the rain,
all that.

Change yourself, modulate your attitude in order to heal
the resentment which will kill you more surely.
Visualize self-autonomies throughout the suburbs,
flower beds encircling rocks. Never mind qualms over

engagement with delusion, if it feels good, yes
have the Qualms over for tea or a barbecue.
Jim and Alice. Bob and Suzie.
The spirit is too grand for petty bourgeois melodramas!
You won't have to think yourself a victim of talentless pretty-
boy actors who become Presidents after losing their looks.
Don't be concerned with the souls of whores
trapped inside men's bodies.
Who controls whom is merely a concept to mull over.

And the bad apples?
After the plucking you can identify them.
They rot more rapidly, in a rush.
Let that be your recompense
when fallen from the tree
into who knows what yard.

February 5, 1995

POEM FOR NEIL

The peculiar human development of the brain, waking up
and finding ourselves organisms in rooms of fancy—
sober museum pieces, fossilized at tea saying *never thought*
he'd seroconvert, survivors
still breathing like a few Victorians—
instead of orgasms in rooms of fantasy
but photography destroyed all that.

None of that getting to know one another in bed
for us anymore!
We've all chosen what we've chosen to be,
and you're too lovely. There, I've confessed it!
With a walk that makes the world shake,
at 25, you've probably already gotten used to
timid ones who phone and hang up.
Be patient with us.

A long history better appreciates what's coming.
The Christians are just getting to a really good disillusionment
of peep-show tokens among spare change and unsafe porn
you can't be in. I'm told I like the neutrality of this space,
the anonymous environment of fog attracts me.
So I'm looking for someone cool from Seattle.
I think I have a name but not a face.
The poem's for you.
I'm not.

May 13, 1995

MISSING

HAVE YOU SEEN THIS MAN?
KARL TIERNEY
POET & FILMMAKER
WHITE MALE
39 YRS. OLD
roughly 6 FEET TALL
around 150 POUNDS
SHORT, BROWN HAIR

Last seen October 13, 1995 in SOMA area of San Francisco

IF YOU HAVE ANY INFORMATION,
PLEASE CALL DAVID AT ███████████

ACKNOWLEDGMENTS & NOTES

Some of these poems made previous appearance as follows:

American Poetry Review: "June 21, 1989" & "Summer Solstice"
Berkeley Poetry Review: "Gertrude Stein to Alice B. Toklas"
Christopher Street: "The Steam Room"
Classical Antiquity: "Caligula or Nixon Leaving" & "Whore"
Crazyquilt Quarterly: "Beauty"
Columbia: "Jinx" and "Mission Dolores"
Contact II: "After His Death"
Court Green: "Part-time Whores in Doorways," "Poem for Neil," &
   "Arkansas Landscape: Wish You Were Here"
Exquisite Corpse: "Dating in a Thinning Field," "Japan," & "Justinian"
Haight Ashbury Literary Journal: "Beauty"
James White Review: "The Blindness of Habit," "Café Hairdo,"
   "Funereal," "Jackie O," "My Alma Mater Honors a Whore of the
   Republic," "Sot," & "Whore"
Mipo: "Adonis at the Swimming Pool," "Hangover," & "White Trash"
modern words: "Boyfriend X Artiste," "Clone Nouveau," & "Skippy"
Opinion Rag: "Billy Idol's Birthday"
Poet News: "What Is There To Do Today?" & "Going Out"
San Francisco Bay Guardian: "Bodybuilder"
San Francisco Sentinel: "Beauty," "Billy Idol's Birthday," "Japan,"
   "Patient Zero," "Summer Solstice," & "The Blindness of Habit"
Skidrow Penthouse: "Brutally Honest," "Club Exile," "Club Uranus,"
   "Easter, 1981," "Nocturne for the Nocturnal," & "The Trees Are
   Wrong"
Whoreson Dog: "Female Dreams"

"After His Death" was published in *Jugular Defences: An AIDS Anthology*
published by Oscars Press, London.

"Funereal," "Gertrude Stein to Alice B. Toklas," "Jackie O," and
"Turning 30" were published in the anthology *Persistent Voices: Poetry
to Writers Lost to AIDS* published by Alyson Books.

"Beauty," "Bed Making," "Billy Idol's Birthday," "Bodybuilder," "Envy," "Going Out," "Jackie O," "Jinx" Summer Solstice," "June 21, 1989," and "The Acquisition of Nothing" were included in *Billy Idol's Birthday*, a chapbook issued in the NEW SINS Chapbook Series, from Pittsburgh, PA, in 1995.

The epigraph to "Billy Idol's Birthday" is unattributed. Research has proven fruitless. The source is a mystery.

Since his death in 1995, a number of individuals and publications have helped keep Karl Tierney's work alive and available to interested readers in print or online form. First and foremost among these is his mother, Karline Tierney, who assisted in assembling an earlier version of this book, furnished photographs, manuscripts and other documentary materials for a forthcoming website and provided continuous moral support and feedback.

Special thanks to the editors of *Skidrow Penthouse*, Rob Cook and Stephanie Dickinson, for including a selection of Karl Tierney poems in Issue #3, Summer, 2000. The introduction to this book first appeared in somewhat different form in that issue under the title "Catullus by the Bay."

CAConrad and Brandon Holmquest offered helpful advice and edits as readers in the early and later, respectively, stages of manuscript evolution.

Among editors and publications, *Exquisite Corpse* and *James White Review* were especially supportive. David Trinidad, in his role as editor of *Court Green*, was also helpful and encouraging in keeping Karl's work before the public. In fact, in 2018, Sibling Rivalry Press publisher Bryan Borland read "Arkansas Landscape: Wish You Were Here" in an old issue of *Court Green*, the catalyst for the publication of this book as part of the Arkansas Queer Poet Series. As with all Sibling Rivalry Press titles, Karl's poems will now be housed for perpetuity alongside history's greatest writers in the Rare Book and Special Collections Vault of the Library of Congress.

ABOUT KARL TIERNEY

Karl Tierney was born in Westfield, Massachusetts, in 1956 and grew up in Connecticut and Louisiana. He became an Eagle Scout in 1973. Poetry fascinated him, even as a teenager. He received a Bachelor's Degree in English from Emory University in 1980 and an MFA in Creative Writing from the University of Arkansas in 1983. That same year, he moved to San Francisco, where he dedicated himself to poetry. He was twice a finalist for the Walt Whitman Award, a finalist for the National Poetry Series, and a 1992 fellow at Yaddo. Though unpublished in book form during his lifetime, his poems appeared in many of the best literary magazines of the period, including the *Berkeley Poetry Review*, *American Poetry Review*, and *Exquisite Corpse*. He published more than 50 poems in magazines and anthologies before his death. In December of 1994, he became sick with AIDS and took his own life in October of 1995. He was 39 years old.

ABOUT JIM CORY

Jim Cory's most recent publications are *Wipers Float In The Neck Of The Reservoir* (The Moron Channel, 2018) and *25 Short Poems* (Moonstone Press, 2016). He has edited poetry selections by contemporary American poets including James Broughton (*Packing Up for Paradise*, Black Sparrow Press, 1998) and Jonathan Williams (*Jubilant Thicket*, Copper Canyon Press, 2005). Poems have appeared recently in *Apiary*, *unarmed journal*, *Bedfellows*, *Cape Cod Poetry Journal*, *Capsule*, *Fell Swoop*, *Painted Bride Quarterly*, *Skidrow Penthouse*, *Trinity Review*, *Have Your Chill* (Australia), and *Whirlwind*. Recent essays have appeared in *Gay & Lesbian Review Worldwide*, *New Haven Review*, and *Chelsea Station*. He has been the recipient of fellowships from the Pennsylvania Arts Council, Yaddo, and The MacDowell Colony. He lives in Philadelphia.

ABOUT SIBLING RIVALRY PRESS

The Arkansas Queer Poet series, proudly published by Sibling Rivalry Press, is dedicated to showcasing LGBTQ poets with a connection to Arkansas. Sibling Rivalry Press is an independent press based in Little Rock, Arkansas. It is a sponsored project of Fractured Atlas, a nonprofit arts service organization. Contributions to support the operations of Sibling Rivalry Press are tax-deductible to the extent permitted by law, and your donations will directly assist in the publication of work that disturbs and enraptures. To contribute to the publication of more books like this one, please visit our website and click *donate*.

Sibling Rivalry Press gratefully acknowledges the following donors, without whom this book would not be possible:

Tony Taylor

Mollie Lacy

Karline Tierney

Maureen Seaton

Travis Lau

Michael Broder & Indolent Books

Robert Petersen

Jennifer Armour

Alana Smoot

Paul Romero

Julie R. Enszer

Clayton Blackstock

Tess Wilmans-Higgins & Jeff Higgins

Sarah Browning

Tina Bradley

Kai Coggin

Queer Arts Arkansas

Jim Cory

Craig Cotter

Hugh Tipping

Mark Ward

Russell Bunge

Joe Pan & Brooklyn Arts Press

Carl Lavigne

Karen Hayes

J. Andrew Goodman

Diane Greene

W. Stephen Breedlove

Ed Madden

Rob Jacques

Erik Schuckers

Sugar le Fae

John Bateman

Elizabeth Ahl

Risa Denenberg

Ron Mohring & Seven Kitchens Press

Guy Choate & Argenta Reading Series

Guy Traiber

Don Cellini

John Bateman

Gustavo Hernandez

Anonymous (12)

CPSIA information can be obtained
at www.ICGtesting.com
Printed in the USA
FSHW020049291019
63502FS